Anne Fine

Valentina Toro

Collins

It could be WORSE

Contents

CHAPTER 1

★ ★ ★ ★ ★

Jamie's mum had a ticket for a raffle and she won first prize. It was two tickets to a big London show, then staying the night in a fine hotel.

She was so happy. "I've always wanted to see this show," she said to Jamie's dad. "All the wonderful singers and dancers. Let's seize the chance and go next week."

"What about me?" asked Jamie. "Can I come with you?"

"I'm sorry, but you can't," said Jamie's mum. "We only have two tickets. And anyway, this is a show for grown-ups."

"But what will *I* do?" asked Jamie.

"There's no problem," said his mother. "You can spend the night with Granny at her house."

Jamie was horrified. "Seriously? All night? By myself?"

"You've stayed at Granny's house before," his dad reminded him.

"Yes," Jamie said. "But you and Mum were there as well."

"Well, this time we won't be," Dad said cheerfully, "because we'll be in London, seeing the show, and staying in the hotel. We'll pick you up when you get out of school the next day."

Jamie hated the plan. It made him feel nervous. He knew that other people in his class stayed over by themselves in other places. He knew that Amy stayed with her grandpa every Wednesday and Friday, when her mother worked all night at the hospital. He knew that Arif often went to stay with his nana and dada – sometimes for whole weekends. And lots of his class had even been on sleepovers with friends. They were quite happy about it. They enjoyed it.

But it's all right for them, thought Jamie. *Some of them do it all the time. They're* used *to it.*

7

But Jamie wasn't used to it.
He'd never, ever done it before, not
without Mum and Dad staying
over as well. And he didn't want to
start now. He wanted to make his
parents change their minds, so he said,
"Suppose I get sick."

"You won't get sick," said Mum.

Jamie tried something else. "Suppose Granny feels too tired to have me."

"She's not an old woman leaning on a stick," his dad said. "She's just your granny, and she has more energy than I do. She won't get tired."

Jamie had one more idea. "Suppose," he said seriously, "that Granny forgets to take me to school in the morning."

His dad shook his head and smiled. "Bad luck! Granny would never forget anything like that!"

10

Oh, it was hopeless. So Jamie thought he might as well tell them what was really worrying him. "What if I get scared?" he said. "What if I hate it?"

"Oh, come on, Jamie!" said his dad. "One night! At Granny's house, where you have stayed before!"

"Not by myself," argued Jamie.

"You won't be by yourself," said Jamie's mum. "You'll be with Granny, and we'll be back the very next day to pick you up from school. And it is just one night. Oh, come on, Jamie. Be brave. It could be worse."

Home Life
The Musical!

Marvel at the speed and elegance of our dusting!

Share the thrill of a morning spent at the bank!

Shudder as our hero unblocks the kitchen sink!

★ ★ ★

These award-winning songs will have you humming all the way home!

★ It's My Turn (To Take the Bins Out)

★ Don't Cry for Me, Window-Cleaner

★ We're All Going Down the Bank

13

Mum and Dad's posh hotel

huge dining room

marble floor

14

CHAPTER 2
★ ★ ★ ★ ★

Only one night! At Granny's house.
But Jamie was still worried. The last
time he went to bed there, he had
a strange experience. He'd heard tiny
voices in his room.

(Next morning, Dad had told him it
was the sound of Granny's radio coming
through the wall, and she'd been
listening to the news.)

And there had been odd bumps and thuds outside his room. (Mum said that it was Cleo the cat, mucking about.)

And every now and again he'd seen ghostly silver lights that slowly snaked over the ceiling and down one of the walls. (Mum and Dad both said they were the headlights of cars as they came round the corner into Granny's street.)

Strange voices. Bumps and thuds. Ghostly silver lights. They were the sort of things that would make anybody nervous. Jamie didn't mind when he knew Mum and Dad were sleeping in the room right next to him.

He could hear all sorts of things that made him feel safe. He could hear his dad saying things like, "Where did I put my pyjamas?" and his mum saying things like, "I hope I haven't forgotten my face cream." It was easy to fall asleep almost as quickly as he would have done back in his own bed at home.

And even if Jamie woke in the middle of the night, he could still hear his dad snoring gently, so he knew that things were all right. He felt quite safe.

But staying at Granny's house without Mum and Dad?

Oh, that was a different matter. Scary!

The days went by. Dad took his suit to the cleaners. Mum found her best silver earrings. And Jamie hoped and hoped that something would happen to make them change their plan to go and see the show.

But nothing did. So, on the day of the show, Mum and Dad came together in the car to pick him up from school and take him over to Granny's house.

They put down his little red overnight bag, and kissed him. "Be good," Mum said. "Enjoy your supper."

"Sleep well," said Dad. "We'll see you tomorrow."

Jamie said nothing so Granny laid a hand on his shoulder. "We'll be just fine," she said. But Jamie didn't feel fine. He hated seeing Mum and Dad get in the car and drive away.

Oh, he liked being with Granny well enough. But he still wished that he was back in his own home, having supper with Mum and Dad exactly as usual, and getting ready to sleep in his own bed.

He tried to be brave and remember what Mum told him. "It could be worse." So, while Granny made supper, Jamie thought a bit more about that.

What could be worse?

Well, they could have left him with someone horrible. *That* would have been worse. They could have left him with a *witch*. And a witch wouldn't be cooking something good, like Granny. A witch would cook a *ghastly* supper. It might have frogs and mice in it. Maybe even worms! He wouldn't want to eat that!

And Mum and Dad had left him for just one night. It could be worse. A whole lot worse. They might have *gone off on a holiday* for two whole weeks.

Yes. It could be worse.

Witch's supper menu

Spooky starters

Slug soup

Mouldy cauliflower salad

Garlic worms

Magical mains

Spaghetti with slime sauce

Roast toad

Bat burger

Dreadful desserts

Frog yoghurt

Baked compost and custard

Toadstool tart

CHAPTER 3

★ ★ ★ ★ ★

It wasn't ghastly frogs and mice
for supper. Or worms. It was Granny's
delicious Mexican pancakes, and as
he was hungry from all the worrying,
Jamie sat down quickly and started
to eat.

After a while, Granny asked him,
"So, Jamie, how was your day in school?"

He was still thinking about the frog and mouse stew he might have been given, so the words just popped out of him. "Oh, it could have been worse."

He saw the startled look on Granny's face. She leant across the table and said, "Could have been *worse*, you say? So was it a *bad* day?"

"No," Jamie said. "It was a good day." He didn't want to explain to Granny that she might have been a witch. He knew that would sound rude. Instead, he said, "I'm just saying that it *could* have been worse. Our school might have burnt down. Or exploded.

Or Mrs Hope might have fallen off her chair and broken both her arms. Or all the books might have been stolen."

Granny gave him a serious look.

"Is that the way you always think about things?" she asked him. "That they could be worse?"

He didn't want his granny to think he was what Mum and Dad called a "worryboots". So, "Oh, no," he told her. "Not at all. I'm only doing it tonight. As a special experience."

"I see," said Granny. And she got up to take the extra Mexican pancakes out of the oven, so they could finish the lot.

After their delicious toffee yoghurt pudding, they played cards. Granny won the first two games and saw Jamie's disappointed face. "It could be worse," she teased. "I could have made you wash all the dishes by yourself, and scrub the floors."

Both of them laughed.

Jamie won the next three games, and Granny made a face. "It could be worse," Jamie told her. "You could have bet me a million pounds that you'd win more games than me."

Both of them laughed again.

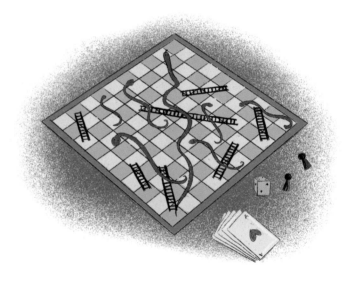

After that, they played Snakes and Ladders. Granny kept landing on the snakes and having to slide down the board. Jamie comforted her. "It could be worse. They could be *poisonous* snakes. Then you would be dead."

After a while, Jamie got right to the second-to-last square, then had to slide down the longest snake on the board. Now it was Granny's turn to comfort him. "It could be worse," she said. "You could have gone down to the bottom over and over again, all through the game, like me."

In the end, Jamie won. Then Granny sent him off to clean his teeth and get into bed. After that, she came in and told him a little about all the people in the photographs in frames on the dresser.

"They were my three great uncles," she said. "William, Alfred and Rupert. They talked to one another for hours on end. They never stopped chatting. Never, ever."

Then she read Jamie a story. It wasn't from the book that Dad was reading to him every night at home. But it could have been worse, because it was a really hilarious story.

Granny put the book back on the dresser next to the photos in the frames, and turned off the bedside lamp. "Night, night," she said. "Sleep tight." And she left the door only a tiny bit open.

CHAPTER 4

★ ★ ★ ★ ★

048211 048211

First, Jamie waited till he was sure that
Granny had returned to the kitchen.
Then he slid out of bed and pushed
the door open a little more. Not so far
that Granny would notice if she walked
past again. But enough to let a bit more
light fall in the room, so it felt less scary.

Then Jamie got back into bed and
bunched up his pillow. Shutting his
eyes, he rolled over.

"Everything's fine," he told himself. "Tomorrow I'll have breakfast with Granny and she might even have remembered I like mushrooms on toast. She might have made sure she has mushrooms." And he wouldn't have to walk to school, as usual, because Granny's house was too far away. He'd get to go in her car, and it had a switch to warm the seat under your bottom. Jamie loved that.

And all the time he was in school he'd know that Mum or Dad, or even both of them, would meet him at the gates to take him home and tell him all about the show and the hotel.

It could be worse.

But then he heard strange tiny voices.
They sounded like the ones Dad told
him came from Granny's radio.

But suppose Dad was wrong!
Dad hadn't slept in Jamie's bed, had he?
He'd been with Mum, in the next room.
Maybe he was just guessing.
Maybe those voices weren't from
Granny's radio at all.

Who could be talking with such teeny
tiny voices?

Teeny tiny people? Creepy!

He thought about the people in
the photos Granny had told him about.
William, Alfred and Rupert. They were
all teeny tiny in the frames. And Granny
had told him that they talked to one
another for hours and hours.

Could they be chatting to each other now, from one photo frame to another? Could *that* be what he was hearing?

Ridiculous! "Absolute nonsense," Jamie told himself sternly. "Photos are just photos. They're not alive and they don't talk."

But the voices kept on. Maybe there were really teeny tiny people somewhere in the room. Maybe they lived hidden in the wall, and only came out at night. Maybe they would climb on his bed and watch him if he fell asleep.

Perhaps he should stay awake? All night! Just in case.

Then, "Nonsense!" he told himself again. "If there are tiny people inside Granny's walls, she'd know about it! In any case, there are no such things as people tiny enough to live in walls. There is nothing to worry about. Dad was right, and Granny is listening to the news."

But the voices still worried him, so he lay very still, and listened very hard, just to be sure that Dad had been right.

And after a while, he found he could hear what the voices were saying. It was dead boring. All about banks and money. Nobody who lived in a wall would care about that stuff, so it must be Granny's radio. Jamie yawned.

A different tiny voice said, "Now for the weather," and it droned on about rain in the north, and showers in the south, and winds in the east, and sunny spells in the west.

"It could be worse," Jamie told himself. "Instead of people on the radio just droning on about money and the weather, Granny could have invited friends round for a party. And all their noisy chatter might have kept me awake, so I'd be exhausted at school in the morning. Yes. It could be worse."

And Jamie snuggled under the covers, to try to go to sleep.

Tiny people in the walls ...

CHAPTER 5
★ ★ ★ ★ ★

Jamie was almost asleep when he
heard the first odd bump outside
his room. And then a thud. And then
another bump. "I mustn't worry,"
he told himself. "Mum says those
bumps and thuds are just Cleo the cat,
mucking about."

He lay and listened.

Thud. Bump. Thud. Bump.

The noises changed a bit.

Biff. Boff. Boff. Biff.

Jamie sat up and looked at the thin line of light shining through the gap in the doorway. He saw a shadow rush across the gap.

Thump. Bump.

He saw the shadow rushing back.

Biff. Boff.

He watched some more. The shadow rushed across the doorway again.

Bump. Thud.

Then it rushed back again
the other way.

Boff. Biff.

Jamie lay back in the bed.
And then he heard a brand new noise.
Scattle. Scuttle. Scuttle. Scattle.

A great heavy lump landed right on
his stomach. "Oof!"

(That last noise was poor Jamie.)

51

The great heavy lump was Cleo.
She had got tired of mucking about
and wanted a short rest. On Jamie.
So she curled herself into a ball and
settled down. Then she began to purr.

Jamie did his best to get comfy again.
It wasn't easy, with a great heavy lump
of cat on him. But he did manage in
the end.

"It could be worse," he
told himself. "Granny could have had
a hippopotamus for a pet. Or even
an elephant. I might have been lying
here for hours, totally squashed.
Oh, yes. It could be worse."

After a bit, Cleo slid off the bed, to
go and sleep with Granny. Jamie rolled
onto his side. At last! Now he could seize
the chance to make himself comfy in
the bed, and get to sleep at last.

But then he saw one of those ghostly
streaks of slinky silver light he'd seen
before snake over the ceiling and down
the wall.

"Dad said that was just car headlights coming round the corner," Jamie told himself. "If Mum and Dad come back tonight, I'll see their lights even before I hear them coming through the door and saying hello to Granny."

They'd said they'd stay at the hotel.

But maybe, thought Jamie, *they changed their minds about going to the show without him. Or maybe the show was cancelled. Perhaps all the singers got sore throats, or flu. Perhaps the dancers all got stuck in a traffic jam. Or went on strike for more money.*

So many things could have happened!
Quite likely one of them would! "I bet
Mum and Dad *do* come back," Jamie
told himself. "I bet the next set of
headlights I see belong to them."

He waited eagerly as the next slinky silver lights snaked over the ceiling. But there were no footsteps up the path. Nobody let themselves in the front door and said hello to Granny.

He tried again. "I bet the third set of headlights I see will be Mum and Dad's."

He waited for more slinky silver lights to snake across the ceiling, and started counting. One ... two ... three ...

Nobody came through the door and said hello to Granny.

"Oh, well," said Jamie. "Maybe they'll be the tenth set of headlights."

Again, he started counting. One ... two ... three ... four ...

CHAPTER 6

★ ★ ★ ★ ★

Jamie woke to see Granny standing, smiling, in the doorway. "Up you get. We mustn't be late for school."

Morning already! And Granny hadn't forgotten to get the mushrooms he loved. When he came into the kitchen, they were already cooked in the pan and all he had to do was butter the toast she had put on his plate.

She piled the mushrooms onto his toast for him, and carried on their game from the night before. "It could be worse," she said. "I could have made you lumpy porridge with sour milk and far too much salt."

"Oh, that's all over now," Jamie said happily. "I don't have to tell myself it could be worse today. All that I have to do today is go to school as usual, have a good day, and Mum or Dad, or even both, will pick me up at the gates."

Granny gave him the biggest smile. "That's good," she said.

Granny ate her usual boiled egg.
When she had finished, she turned
the shell over in the egg cup, and gave it
to Jamie to put a silly face on it.

Jamie used one of the felt pens in his
school bag to draw big flapping ears
and long scruffy hair on the eggshell.
Then he picked up the little red overnight
bag that Granny had packed his stuff in,
and followed her out to the car.

It wasn't cold, but still he used
the button that made the seat warm,
just for fun. The traffic wasn't bad,
and Granny dropped him off at
the school gates.

"Have a good day," she said.
"And don't forget your Dad or Mum will
pick you up, as usual."

"Or even both of them," said Jamie. He pushed down the handle to let himself out of the car. He couldn't think why he was feeling so happy. And then he realised that, just like Amy and Arif, and all of the other people in the class who had had sleepovers, he'd spent the night away from home without his Mum and Dad.

And he'd had fun. He had been worried by the tiny voices. And by the scary bumps and thuds. And by the strange, ghostly lights that snaked across the ceiling. But he hadn't just been a worryboots.

He'd been brave and sensible, even though he was all by himself. He'd gone to sleep, and was ready for a full day at school. And he was really looking forward to seeing Mum and Dad and hearing all about the show and the hotel.

Jamie turned round to smile at Granny. He remembered what he'd been told to say, to be polite. "Thank you for having me," he said.

And then he added something all of his own. "And can I come and stay with you again?" he asked. "All by myself? For the whole night? Without Mum and Dad?"

"You certainly can," said Granny.

So he did.

Next sleepover at Granny's
(by Jamie)

We could ...

- invite Arif to sleep over too

- climb the big tree in the park

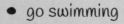

- go swimming

- play video games

- have Mexican pancakes for supper (of course!)

- have cocoa and marshmallows

- stay up REALLY late!

- sleep over for TWO nights!

"It could be worse" game

You can play this game with a friend.
Take turns to think of something bad that
could happen.

Bad thing
You don't
like your
packed lunch.

Bad thing
You're late
for school.

Bad thing
It's raining
at playtime.

Bad thing
You left your
book bag
at home.

Bad thing
You've got
a cold.

The other person has to think of a way that it could be worse. Here are some ideas to start you off!

It could be worse ...
A monster might have eaten it.

It could be worse ...
At least you got there in the end.

It could be worse ...
It could be worm sandwiches.

It could be worse ...
At least there isn't an earthquake.

It could be worse ...
At least you haven't got blue-spotted bogeyitis.

About the author

How did you get into writing?

I was always a madly keen reader, but once, kept from the library by a blizzard, I started to write my own book, and I never stopped.

Is there anything in this book that relates to your own experiences?

Anne Fine

I was used to sharing a bedroom and, with my elder sister beside me, I always felt safe. I once spent three nights with my grandparents, and I was terrified. Strange noises, strange lights, strange smells — strange everything. In the end, I'd fall asleep from sheer exhaustion.

What do you hope readers will get out of the book?

Everything new can be testing for young people. But you can learn from people in books. You, as the reader, think, "He has no reason to be scared at all," or, "She must know she's just inventing scary things." Stories help you work out how you'd feel in that position. Then, if it happens, some of your thinking has stuck, and you are better prepared.

Did you ever go on a sleepover when you were young? Were you scared of anything?

I was at least 12 before I had a sleepover I enjoyed, with my best friend at school. And even then, I didn't feel all that confident. Her parents seemed very strange to me – though probably only because they weren't a bit like mine.

Anything else you'd like to say?

When I was three, my mother had triplets, so I was sent to the infant school next door along with my five-year-old sister, mostly for babysitting. (Things were less formal in those days.) Nobody explained to me, so I just learnt to read along with all the rest and carried on up the school, year by year.

The primary school refused to take me till I was seven, so I had to stay where I was. The only thing they made me do over again was Arithmetic (which we called "Sums"). The rest of the time I was given free run of all the school's bookshelves, and for a whole year I was just left to read at the back of the class with my fingers stuck in my ears. What bliss! And since the practice for being a writer is not writing, but reading, just guess what happened?

About the illustrator

A bit about me ...

I'm from Colombia, the most biodiverse country in the world, and that's why I've always loved to draw animals and plants. My biggest passions are reading, drawing and walking my dog. I have been writing and illustrating

Valentina Toro

children's books for over ten years now. I have a disability and my service dog's name is Yeti.

What made you want to be an illustrator?

I always loved bedtime stories, but what I loved the most were the pictures from the books that my mum used to read to me. One day I realised that I couldn't stop thinking about them and that I was always imagining new stories full of pictures of my own. So that's when I decided that I wanted to spend my life between pencils and stories.

How did you get into illustration?

My dad is an illustrator too, a pretty good one, and he was my first teacher and the one that showed me the path.

What did you like best about illustrating this book?

I love the characters and the imagination that Jamie has.
I felt related right away.

What was the most difficult illustration?

The one with the tiny voices from the wall, because it's such
a mysterious and lovely idea that you don't want to mess it up.

**Is there anything in this book that relates to your
own experiences?**

Yes. I was easily scared as a child, and I was always making
up funny stories in my head.

How do you bring a character to life?

I always try to catch their personality somehow ... I try to
think about how they move, how they interact with each
other and how their facial expressions are going to manifest
their true personality. Sometimes it's not about their outfits or
accessories, but their faces and their bodies and the way they
inhabit the story with movement and independence.

Do the characters look like people you know?

I didn't notice it at first, but when I made the first sketches
of the three gentlemen from the frames in Granny's spare
room, I ended up drawing three people similar to my own
grandfather and his brothers.

Book chat

Which character did you like best, and why?

Did your mood change while you were reading the book? If so, how?

Which scene stands out most for you? Why?

If you had to give the book a new title, what would you choose?

Which part of the book did you like best, and why?

Did this book remind you of anything you have experienced in real life?

If you could change one thing about this book, what would it be?

Do you think Jamie changed between the start of the story and the end? If so, how?

Book challenge:

Design your perfect sleepover.

Collins
BIG CAT

Published by Collins
An imprint of HarperCollins*Publishers*

The News Building
1 London Bridge Street
London SE1 9GF
UK

Macken House
39/40 Mayor Street Upper
Dublin 1
D01 C9W8
Ireland

10 9 8 7 6

ISBN 978-0-00-862460-6

British Library Cataloguing-in-Publication Data
A catalogue record for this publication is
available from the British Library.

Download the teaching notes and
word cards to accompany this book at:
http://littlewandle.org.uk/signupfluency/

Get the latest Collins Big Cat news at
collins.co.uk/collinsbigcat

Author: Anne Fine
Illustrator: Valentina Toro (Advocate Art)
Publisher: Lizzie Catford
Product manager: Caroline Green
Series editor: Charlotte Raby
Development and commissioning
    editor: Catherine Baker
Project manager: Emily Hooton
Phonics reviewer: Rachel Russ
Content editor: Daniela Mora Chavarría
Copyeditor: Sally Byford
Proofreader: Gaynor Spry
Typesetter: 2Hoots Publishing Services Ltd
Cover designer: Sarah Finan
Production controller: Katharine Willard

Collins would like to thank the teachers and
children at the following schools who took part in
the trialling of Big Cat for Little Wandle Fluency:
Burley And Woodhead Church of England
Primary School; Chesterton Primary School; Lady
Margaret Primary School; Little Sutton Primary
School; Parsloes Primary School.

Printed and bound in the UK

MIX
Paper | Supporting
responsible forestry
FSC™ C007454
www.fsc.org